John Vance Cheney

**Queen Helen**

And Other Poems

John Vance Cheney

**Queen Helen**
*And Other Poems*

ISBN/EAN: 9783744705141

Printed in Europe, USA, Canada, Australia, Japan

Cover: Foto ©Thomas Meinert / pixelio.de

More available books at **www.hansebooks.com**

# QUEEN HELEN

## AND OTHER POEMS

### BY

## JOHN VANCE CHENEY

CHICAGO

WAY & WILLIAMS

1895

# QUEEN HELEN

## PERSONS

MENELAUS, *King of Sparta.*
HELEN, *his Queen.*
PARIS, *Prince of Ilion.*
ÆTHRA, *serving-woman to the Queen.*
*Courtiers of Sparta.*
*Courtiers of Ilion.*

*Scene:* SPARTA.

# CONTENTS

# QUEEN HELEN

Palace of Menelaus.
The King and Queen looking from a window.

*Menelaus.*

Who are the stranger-folk the people crowd
About, and lead up hither from the river?

*Helen.*

More hunters, come to boast, and chase the boar
With Menelaus, Sparta's hunter-king.

*Menelaus.*

And Helen's husband.

*Helen.*

Hence he should not hunt,
Forsake her bed for dens and lairs of beasts.
Fame does not trump my lord as Helen's husband;
Yon rovers rove not after any husband,
Their chariots thunder toward the hunter-king.

*Menelaus.*

Came they to me because I wear the pearl
Of all the world upon my breast, then were
This house a fiercer den than any on
Taygetus.   We should sit a throne of bones,
And drink our wine from cups of carvéd skulls.
Nay, nay, my golden girl, wherefore so pale?
It was but play.

*Helen.*

I do not use to see
That look. 'T is gone, and with it my silly fright.

*Menelaus.*

The leader is no Greek.   We Grecians walk
The ground; my Prince, there, trips it on the wind.
They are come in.   Rest, girl, you are not well.

[Exit.

*Helen.*

Is it the wand of Hermes?   Do I sleep?

2

No Greek, indeed; what was the shape I saw,
And what the glory flashed, and hid him in 't?


Palace Hall.　Menelaus and Courtiers.　Paris and Courtiers.

### Paris.

King Menelaus, we are of Ilion all,
Turned from our errand.　Not with men it lies,
But with the gods, to reach the wished-for shore.
Our baffled sails were set for Salamis ;
Yonder they flap, down by the Spartan strand.
Float whitherward we may, we hail from Thrace,
Where built my grandsire, old Laomedon,
Poseidon and Apollo both his slaves
For the strong work.

### Menelaus.

　　　　　You are good Priam's son.
Come, let me take you by the hand.　We know
Your white-haired father well, fair spoken of fame ;
Know Hecabe's first-born, your brother, Hector ;
And fortune now has added fair young Paris,
Ay, given us leave to look him in the face.
Most welcome !

3

*Paris.*

Menelaus locks my tongue,
Which should declare the purpose of our journey.

*Menelaus.*

Speak on ; but plain the look of these my friends,
Intent on further service, bids me say
You shall not go till we have faced the boar
Together, and so tried the thews of Thrace.

*Paris.*

Most willingly we bide a little time,
At least till we have hunted, and have pledged
Cups from the fragrant hills round Ismaron.
Longer we may not stay ; for we are sent,
As will be granted, on an urgent journey.
When Heracles laid low Laomedon,
He took for spoil his child, Hesione,
And gave her to his friend, Prince Telamon
Of Salamis.   Prince Telamon, as all
Men know, is dead, and in his place reigns Ajax.
So now it stands that my old father's sister
Is pining captive in a stranger-land,
Exiled and base dishonored.   Wherefore we
Are charged to go to Salamis and say,
" Priam would have Hesione at home."

4

### Menelaus.

'T is a just mission.   We will feast to-night,
And hunt to-morrow.   Rested from the hunt,
As squares it with your pleasure you shall sail,
Commissioned doubly strong: "Ilion and Sparta
Demand of Salamis old Priam's sister."

Banquet-Hall.   Menelaus leads in Helen.

### Menelaus.

It were no banquet not set off with Helen.
Our ways are freer, Prince, than they may be
At Ilion.   Ere we fall to baser joys,
My Queen, receive our new friend Paris, who,
If he but bide a week, when he departs
Will take with him the heart of love-sick Sparta.

### Æthra.   [Aside.

If my old eyes can see, it will be so ;
If my old hands can help, it shall be so.

### Paris.

Most gracious lady, light of Lacedæmon,
In honest Sparta none may hide his thought.

*Æthra.* [Aside.

Tush, Paris! Aphrodite's thought, not yours.

*Paris.*

It happened, once, on a slope of piny Ida,
There came unto a shepherd lad, who fed
The flocks of my old father, ladies three
That walk the envied ways of blest Olympus.
The Olympian gallants, gods although they are,
High born as they themselves, could not, it seems,
Be trusted to decide which was the fairest.
They found the herdboy on Scamander's bank—
Scamander, yellow as his own wild locks,
Stained with the sunshine.   There he sat, and
        played
As blithe a pipe as ever lifted foot
Of faun or forest nymph, dancing to Pan.
The first to speak was she that sits by Zeus,
The Bride of Heaven : "Sweet lad, we know that
        you,
Lovelier than are the lovely things you live
Among,—the brooks, the blossoms, and the
        trees,—
Can truly tell of thousand beauteous shapes
Which is most beautiful.   Take you this apple,
And, looking on us justly, give it her

6

You find the fairest." "Glossy boy," spoke then
She with the oval face and floating hair,
The virgin 'gainst whose ivory side the lance
Of love is shattered, she whose glowing shoulder
Smote once poor mortal sight, and put it out
Forever,—"take it, boy, and with free hand
Offer it her whose right it is. Decide ;
We stand upon the choice."
Till now the lad stood gazing ; dazed, but bent
To do his best with what few thoughts were left.
He stood there, tapping with the reed his limbs
Well plumped, yet trembling under him, he felt,
When the other moved toward him, drew very
        close,
And, silent, waited. He looked up at her,
And, as a wondering child wakes out of sleep,
And reaches toward its waiting mother, so
He waked, and put the apple in her hand.
Could he do otherwise? This last it was
That rose from the pure foam by blossomy Cyprus,
And slipt like summer morning down the shore,
Which, printed soft with her immortal feet,
Sent roses up and lilies as she went.


*Æthra.* [Aside.

Let him step forth that had done otherwise.

7

## Helen.

It is a pretty tale; but, Prince, your thought?

## Paris.

Poor silly, silly lad!

## Helen.

I think his elders had not hit it better.

## Paris.

He stopt not with the deed, but would stout hold,
When ripe his years were grown, that he had
    looked
Upon the fairest shape of man or god.
So late he learns the cheat: I was that boy.

## Menelaus.

Dread Prince, see that you bide within my walls.

## Æthra.   [Aside.

Fecks! he will be obedient; never fear.

## Menelaus.

Though Zeus were for it, I 'd not let you loose
Among the listening girls.  Had I your tongue,
Though horrent bodied as the monster hewn
To 's death by blue-eyed Heracles at foot

Of Ilion's towers, I swear I could go forth
And ravish all the darlings of mankind,
Nor leave one love for him that followed me.

### Paris.

Your lord lets rise my raw, unordered words,
With marshaled Spartan ranks to march them
    down.
Pray, lady, take this gold, these jewels, worth
A little kingdom, and, comparing them
With what I gave to Aphrodite, know
The man is so much wiser than the boy.
And you, O King, who, by some art beyond
Rude Ilion's reach, have won this lady, take
For badge of victory a suit of gold,—
This armor wrought to case a kingly shape,
And with it grasp this fitting spear, to guard
Your god's possession 'gainst the emptied world.


First Group of Courtiers, in another part of the room.

### First Spartan.

Come, now, have Ilion's meadows all the bees,
And has your prince drained every hive?

### First Trojan.
                      That 's Paris.

9

*Second Trojan.*

Fear not for him that from his cradle mates
With Cebren nymphs, and, fair as they themselves,
Has many loves as he has sunny days.

Second Group of Courtiers.

*First Spartan.*

Oft as I 've blinked upon the shining queen,
Always before I could half ope my eyes ;
To-night I 'm blind as old Tiresias.

*Second Spartan.*

Take you his blindness ; I prefer his seership.
Comes there not something of that parley such
As men to furthest time will not forget,
I am no prophet.

*First Spartan.*

   Much is settled now :
Before this hour eye has not seen two mortals
Together, bright as yonder pair. So soft
As Argive Helen's look was not her own
That out of heaven leaned, and straight was lost
To it in shadows of the Latmian bower ;
Nor he that drew her down knew sweeter dream
Than folds, now, raptured Paris.

*Third Spartan.*

Menelaus,
If you do sleep, to-night, in wonted peace,
I 'll not believe you Agamemnon's brother.

First Group of Courtiers.

*Trojan.*

We jest ; the prince but plays a merry part,
The queen but hears, and answers him in kind.

*Spartan.*

Nay, man, I think the queen much moved withal.
And, I would ask once more, why is it women,
Or high or low, so droop on dainty men,
Falling in love, as 't were, among themselves ?

*Trojan.*

You wrong the prince.   His leopard's lines, his
        head,
So bright, and airy carried, work deceit ;
His are the thews that, next to Hector's, bend
The necks of Thrace.

*Spartan.*

A thousand pardons, Thracian,
But 't is the very hardest thing of all
For my belief.

11

*Trojan.*

                    To-morrow, should the chase
Be worth it, you will see another man
Than he, there, dallying with the dreamy queen.


*Spartan.*

To-night thrive Ilion,—feasting and fair women ;
To-morrow Sparta,—fasting and dumb valor.


*Trojan.*

But see, the queen retires, led lingering off
In loveliness which, after all, goes not,
But, like a summer day, disputes the dark.


*Another Spartan.*

Now to our cups, and pleasures meet for men,
Then sleep, if time be left ; and when first snort
The horses of the morning, for the hills,
And Sparta's joy, cropping the flower of Ilion.


*Another Trojan.*

The tenderest flower sometimes has hardy stem,
And oft, too, from its softness sticks a thorn.
So let it rest ; for yonder he returns

Under whose royal roof no noise should break
Save sounds of praise and honest revelry.

Paris, alone on his couch, after the banquet.
Æthra approaches him.

### Æthra.

Young Prince, I am a woman, neither nymph
Nor maid love-led from lorn Scamander's bank.
Prince, I am old; I was not always so.
Years ere you breathed the air or charmed the hearts
Of Ilion, I was young.  The years change all,
What is, to-day, shows nothing of what was ;
You meet me here, silvered and bent, a slave,
Shorn even of the honor due white hairs.

### Paris.

Woman, you have my pity.   Is 't for that
You come, when age with youth should covet sleep?

### Æthra.

Sleep !   Had I your youth and what the gods
Have given you with it, placed as you are, now,
My eyes, instead of folding in blank lids,

Would stare themselves from out their tortured
    sockets.
Pity for my poor self? Nay, but for her,
The child-wife Helen. I have not forgot,
Though 't be so far behind, how sweet youth is.
To Sphæria, on the gulf of Saron, once
I fared, fleet as the wind. Under a cliff
With awful shadow was I secret bathing,
When from his palace, in the splendid deep
By rocky Imbros, drave Poseidon forth
His horses golden-hoofed and brazen-maned,
And lashed them toward his palace on the shore.
His fierce glance pierced to me; he reached, and
    off
His chariot whirled us. Ay, Poseidon 't was.
I tell you this that you may know how much
It is I say, as on my knees I swear
The water-god caught up a freckled wench
Compared to her the prey of laggard Paris.


### Paris.

Woman, I am the guest of Menelaus.


### Æthra.

Has love, in truth, become so poor! Why, love,
It owned the world when I was young; ay, had

14

There been a thousand worlds, it would have ranged
'Em all, and brought their haughty riches home
To deck its pleasure-house and bridal bed.
There was no king but love, no queen but beauty,
In days when virgins closed with kings and gods,
And sons were born were worth the weight and
        pain,
Sons that, as babes, would grasp the father's spear,
And shake 't in play as no man swings it now.

### Paris.

Did all the world turn robber, he'd not fall
With it, the guest of her so honest lord.

### Æthra.

Honest, spotless Atreides!
Believe it, scorn the gods, and get you hence
With two dead hearts for trophy. two dead lives,
Two loves that might have been, sweeter than loves
That make men pale to read of, vilely slain.

*Aphrodite appears, and vanishes.*

### Paris.

Wild as my thought plunges no bolt of Jove,
Driven, hissing, down the hollow of the night. —
I do not sleep ; say on.

It is sound sleep to what 't will turn ere long ;
I have borne sons, and know the stuff of men.
How came he by her, he, the blameless king ?
When Helen yet was in her bud of beauty,
Foreseeing the blossom of her summertime,
Came up the suitors to old king Tyndareus —
Her sister's father, Paris, not her own,
As I in time will show you — till his gate
Was full.   Cretan Idomeneus came up,
His chariot clogged with gold ; Meges was here,
The son of Phyleus, brave as the battle-god ;
Antilochus, the young and bold, pressed in,
With melody stolen from his snowy sire,
Who speaks, and charms the very winds of Pylos ;
By him his rival, he of Ithaca,
Odysseus, cunning as the serpents round
Apollo's shrine.   Next him horseman Menestheus,
Who rolled 'gainst Theseus his mad chariot
        wheels,
And haled him basely from his father's throne ;
Here Diomedes strode, behind his shield,
Ward of the bluest eyes that watch from heaven ;
And to and fro among them all would pass
Methone's prince, the friend of Herakles,
Who took from him his arrows as he died.

*Paris.* [To himself.

I know not why, I shuddered at that last.

*Æthra.*

As I have named them came they up that, side
By side with Menelaus, chafed these walls
Which shut us in, to-night, shouldering toward
     Helen.
You picture gentle, high-born gardeners, come
To pluck, ere it should flower, the Spartan bud.
I tell you, I, who faced them, man by man,
They were so many bulls,
Which locked their horns together, pawed the
     ground
As they would plow away Eurota's shore,
Bellow strong Sparta down, till one of all
Should lure the heavenly heifer from her hills.
It thaws the winter in my veins to think on 't ;
And your young blood, young summer blood,
     instead
Of throbbing hot to valor's fiery top,
Does clot and scum in the dull ooze of sleep.

*Paris.* [Mutters, his mind returning to the vision.

It was the smile, the very smile, she gave
When I looked up at her, shining on Ida.

## Æthra.

The prize that felled all Greece at Sparta's feet,
Was 't honorably won, at last? 'T was tossed
By lot into the lap of Menelaus.
He has her, Paris—and he has her not.
I say it over : I have been a girl,
And for a girl I speak.

## Paris. [Rousing.

Woman, I am his guest. And saw I not,
A little hour ago, she loves the king?
She has waxed fond of him, wooed by sure worth,
Than which a better lover never was.

## Æthra.

With but a glance young Paris can see more
Than Æthra with her years, with all her days
And nights of watching, close as fondest mother
To nestling Helen. Not a thought is hers
But I can hear it. So, from childhood, has
It been ; her little troubles all my own,
Ay, all her bitter sorrows and her joys.
Hence, well as I hate the blackened line of Atreus,
So well I love the unsullied girl. I love
Her, Paris, else I should not parley more,
But leave you both to take the meed of them

That scorn the guerdon of the eternal gods,
And, beggars, shamble, ragged, down to death.

>                    *Paris.*   [Fiercely.

She loves the king.

>                    *Æthra.*

>                    Ay, since who has her heart
Is monarch of all men, the very king.

>                    *Paris.*

She loves her lord.

>                    *Æthra.*

>                    Ay, since who has her love
Is so her lord.—Didst ever know a nurse
So put to 't she came off without her story?
You and your train had just come in the hall,
And Menelaus gone to greet you, when,
As wont, I went to bind young Helen's hair.
Upon her couch I found her, fallen asleep
As soft and soon as babe upon the breast.
Asleep she was, yet would she smile, yea, speak,
At times, deep in most wondrous rapture.  Then
Did I divine 't was not a common sleep,
But a sweet spell laid on her.  When she woke—
It was not long—she yet stayed half in sleep,
Nor spoke she more than, now and then, a word,
Which sounded like a bird-tone far away,

Adrift in the mid-forest.  So it happed
As you approached the palace.  While I robed
The girl, to-night, she plied me,—"Æthra, how
May mortals tell when truly 't is a god ;
Whether it be a dream, or they in truth
Look on a very god ?"  I answered her,
It was a thing to learn of one's own self,
Not to be taught.  "I think, I think," she said—
Ah, Paris, had you heard her say it, seen
The dreamy lids droop half-way down her eyes !—
"I think the prince is followed by a goddess."

### Paris.

Go, now, hoar Æthra ; I had rather dream
Most frightful things that rack their souls in Hell
Than let this lead me further.

### Æthra.

           'T is enough.
If so the goddess bring you sleep, fall off ;
If so she bid you wake, stand to the watch ;
I will not pit my wisdom 'gainst Olympus.
But this I do command you, by my might
Of prophet's blood, and by my many years,
And by the memory of my youth and beauty,
And by my love, the guard of darling Helen,
Hold stiff your spear, to-morrow.
                    [Exit.

## Paris.

'T was an old woman's tale, all known before,
So straight the sight of love.—Benignant goddess,
Oh, Aphrodite, thou hast kept thy word!
Could I be deaf to those two wailing voices,
The voice of wild Œnone, my boyhood's love,
And the voice of her, my sister, wan Cassandra ;
Could I shut out their cries,— "Go not, go not!"
"O Paris, bring not back with thee a wife!"
Did not these cries torment me, I should sink
To sleep soft as the lovely Helen slept,
Dear Goddess, on thy breast.
Man walks in darkness, none can see the way ;
But thou wilt open it to me as I go.
To-night, I ask but this : fend envious Heaven
From me, to-morrow. Gods will watch my steps
From this hour on, to make me slip. Ward off
The gods. Against no mortal crave I aid.


*Helen.* [Alone, weaving and singing.

Softly, shepherd, watch your flock,
They must let the baby rock,—
By-a-baby, by-a-by ;

Keep the dreams back, every one,
Till the journey is begun.
By-a-baby, by-a-by.

Not till baby floats away,
Pretty shepherd, let them stray,—
By-a-baby, by-a-by;
Then around him let them play;
Hark, you, shepherd, what I say.
By-a-baby, by-a-by.

Careless shepherd, keep them back;
One is coming, white and black,—
By-a-baby, by-a-by;
Never, never let him go
That has spot upon his snow;
By-a-baby, by-a-by.

Softly, shepherd, soft, I say,
Not till baby floats away,—
By-a-baby, by-a-by.
Ah, the dreamkins, well they know!
Loose them, shepherd, let them go:
All alone are you and I.


Enter Menelaus, returned from the hunt.

### *Menelaus.*

Fair as the dream the nimble thread shall fix,
Slipping from those deft fingers, gliding on
That wild-bird melody.

*Helen.*

My lord come home !
Safe, and a full day sooner than he said.

*Menelaus.*

Home, dearest, hardly safe ; mark you this mark.
And lucky man I am it is no worse.

*Helen.*

The king will have his war ; when there 's no war
Will make it ; tusk of boar will take for spear
Wielded by direst foe of mortal breed,
And dash against it, and get grievous wounds,
As he were battling for his queen and kingdom.

*Menelaus.*

Sweet girl ! forever finding precious fault —

*Helen.*

Which halts yet far behind your true desert —

*Menelaus.*

Which is more sweet to hear than song of nymphs,
Tripping in grove and glen.

*Helen.*

It is more praise
Than blame, or Menelaus could not wake it.

A palace can be lonely — let it go.
But I do hate the boars!  Is 't a bad hurt?

### Menelaus.

The best hurt 's bad.   For cure I 'll take a peep
Into the fairy secret of your loom.

### Helen.  [Holding him back.

Not yet ;  the charm 's at work.

### Menelaus.

                                    Well, tell me, then,
What song you sang.    That may a little help me.

### Helen.

A sleep-song Æthra taught me long ago,
A lullaby one hears at Athens, where
Over the door the olive wreath has hung.
It came to me as I thought on my childhood.
But 't is an ugly gash!   Now will I heal it,
Do 't sooner than the eldest of my women ;
Here be my ointments and my bandages.
I hope you wreaked upon the brute revenge
So fierce, the news of it will spread till all
Wild Theras howls at Menelaus' name.

*Menelaus.*

My loud war-cry was as a summer breath,
Nor carried it more terror.

*Helen.*

A noble foe, his every bristle kingly !
Would I might gloat on him, a humble captive.

*Menelaus.*

A joy, I question not, to every woman ;
The tusk that dealt me this was grown in Thrace.

*Helen.*

A Thracian monster did it ! Point him out,
To-night, when I will drive him to the prince,
And get his price, that we may keep him, cage
Him up, against a merry hunt at home.

*Menelaus.*

Keep him ! Nay, that were harder fortune yet ;
Next would he wound my queen, work her such
　　hurt
As not her skill and mine, combined, could medi-
　　cine ;
'T was Paris' taper hand that dealt the blow.

### Helen.

The prince! I 'd risk my naked arm 'gainst his.

### Menelaus.

The courage is too common ; boast not on 't.

### Helen.

The prince! nay, say 't was some one 'mong my
  maids.
Paris, the soft, the silken !

### Menelaus.

Ay, that same Paris, with a woman's wrist
And ringlets.   Never more misleading man
Did ramp Taygetus' lairs.   To see him lilt
Along the hills, swinging this way and that
As though a zephyr steered him, then the change
When 't came to make a stand ! Four of us
  rushed
Together to stop as huge a brute as scours
The mountain.   I was first ; but, in the nick,
Before me leapt the prince, who drew, and gave
Me one spear-end the while the brute took t'other,
Pricked to quick death.   Beware o' silken princes !

### Helen.

Forthwith dispatch him ; Sparta is not safe.

### Menelaus.

Nay, hear me, girl : I have not met the man
I 'd rather make my friend.   He shall not go,
But tarry with us long as pleasure holds him.
To-morrow, I set out.   Till my return
Hold fast Prince Paris.

### Helen.

           I had thought, perhaps,
You would deny, for once, Idomeneus,
And let the restless Cretans chase alone.
One day the king will hunt one day too many.

*Enter Æthra.*

### Menelaus.

'T is one of haggard Æthra's midnight mutterings.
Play not the prophet, girl ;  be a brave queen.
One has his friends, and has one friend of all ;
I never can refuse Idomeneus.
However, I will cut my pleasure short ;
Meanwhile be generous with our Thracian guests,
Deal with free hand ;  in nothing stint the prince,
Make him to feel that all I have is his.

*Æthra.*  [Aside.

If he do feel 't not, now, Olympus is
Untopped, and all the gods are tumbled down.


Helen at her loom, Æthra by her side.

### *Æthra.*

Heyday! the king is off; it 's hunt again,
And woman rules once more unsinewed Sparta.
What said his kingship when you showed him
    that?

### *Helen.*

'T is but begun; I could not show it so.

### *Æthra.*

What is the name o' 't?

### *Helen.*

        Name? There 's naught to name
As yet.  First have the thing, when it will speak,
And name itself.

### *Æthra.*

        The posture is a god's,
Confronting, I may say, a Spartan palace;

28

And that above his head, which first I took
For cloud, may grow into a goddess' wings.

### Helen.

'T is faithful if so quick you make it out.

### Æthra.

A jump, and lo, your skill is at the pitch :
A wondrous sudden mount.   One power, but
   one,
My lass, can push so fast.   You have the thing,
And so, as you have taught me, have its name :
Therefore I need not speak it.

### Helen.
                         After all,
It may not be the prince.

### Æthra.

                      The king, perhaps,
Hung round with hunter's glory.

### Helen.
                         Æthra, how
Can you love Helen so well, and hate so hard
Helen's honest husband?   What does help my
   heart,

Give it a little play, too much shut in,
Might hurt his heart, which has more room than
    mine.
He wrongs you, truly, holding you in Sparta ;
But it is for my sake.


*Æthra.*
            I will requite
His service yet.   If he is king, know I
Too, had, one time, a kingdom.   You forget
Who Æthra is ; what moves me more, forget
Who Helen is.   Is she the king's or love's?
Think back, my Queen, and prick the silly bubbles.
In this same room where now you picture him
That is the very king, striving to lift
Him from your heart, and hold him for your eyes
To see even as your heart sees,—in this room,
I say, forgetful Helen, love, long since,
Enjoyed a queen, or you were not here, now.
In at that window flew the sovereign swan
That, shadowing your mother, quicked her with
    love
That love might be again.   You are that love ;
And, sure as Zeus upholds his throne, the king
Of love will claim his own.   So soon he comes.

Enter Paris, while Helen hurriedly covers the loom.

### Paris.

And why should I not see how prospers art
At Sparta?

### Helen.

       'T is scarce swaddled yet ; the face,
Of him whose rude arm well nigh overthrew
My husband, wielded but in silly sport,
Would fright my youngling past the hope of
    growth.

### Æthra. [Aside.

That 's lamer than Hephæstus : he whose face,
At the first flash o' 't, overwhelmed the queen,
With her the king, and with the twain the king-
    dom.

                      [Exit Æthra.

### Paris.

Who is the woman with Queen Helen so much,
This moment gone?

### Helen.

           Prince, I half shame to tell.
For, once a queen, a queen, say I, forever.
Æthra, a slave at Sparta, was a queen
At home.   The chance of battle lodged her here,
And here she bides.  Myself would set her free;

But since the king's will runs the other way,
She stays to serve me.

*Paris.*

Can you trust her, Queen?

*Helen.*

As surely as great Pittheus was her sire,
The prophet-king.

*Paris.*

A royal prophetess !

*Helen.*

Yet blind enough with love to serve too well.

*Paris.*

Now first I learn that love may love too well.

*Helen.*

In truth it may.   Love is too greedy, fierce.
Love must have all or nothing ;
A furious path it takes, to follow it
Through bloody seas and wastes ablaze with war.
I think the poets praise love much too much,
And with it that other, beauty.   Yes, these two,
So famed, I deem of doubtful worth.   Could I

Be born anew, and have my own poor making,
I 'd be a man, a slow man and content,
One not to move or to be moved on slight
Occasion ; one would know the greatest is
But small, that he is favored most whose place
Is only large enough for him and peace ;
Yes, Prince, him would I be, that model man.

### Paris.

The gods be thanked they had their way, not
    yours !

### Helen.

I would not blame the gods, though I must feel,
At times, they work us wrong.  To it I cling:
Love is the very maddest might in all
This stormy world ; and beauty, could it choose
'Twixt praise and pity, oft would take the pity.

### Paris.

Were I the king, I 'd send old Æthra home,
And rid my queen of such philosophy
As flies i' the face of nature.

### Helen.
                Lay it not
At Æthra's door ; hers are quite other thoughts.
But now, enough ; we enter shadowy ways,

Which none should ever walk in till he must.
'T was you, grave Prince, that led; the fault is
    yours.

### Paris.

Queen Helen, do you play with me, or toward
Your heart creeps the black shadow on mine own?
I question if again the sun will shine
For me, ay, if my night will burn one star.
As gods and all men know, none sees your face
And loves you not.   I, that was born for love,
And, as you say too truly, born likewise
To fire and blood of war—I, Queen, so born,
The last of men can look into your face,
And be thereafter what I was.   I came
As light of life as any flower that nods
In Ceres' fields; I take me hence as weighed
As the pine that, blasted, hangs his pithless arms,
Lone, on the windy cliff.
'T is not the time or place for me to speak;
But you will speak, for one thing must I know.
Queen Helen, if you meant your life is now
Happier than it would be held close in love
Fixed as the star is fixed in the pure heavens;
If, verily, you meant that, tell me so.
Tell me, and I 'll not speak another word.
And, oh, if 't was but said, not meant, again

I pray you, tell me so! The time is short :
This night my sail shall fill for Salamis.

### Helen.

So soon! My lord will not forgive me for it.

### Paris.

Yes, Queen, to-night. My men are in the boats.

### Helen.

The nights are many, many ; why to-night?

### Paris.

My men await the signal ; I, your answer.
Be open with me, that I may know if now
I look my last on this eternal beauty,
Or tear me from it, vowing to return,
Prepared to speak my love, and make it good
At point of Trojan swords.

### Helen.

You said to-night, and something after that.
I have a dizziness, at times ; I hear,
I hear, yet do not hear.— Was that good Æthra?

*Æthra*.   [Entering.

Ay, little Helen Queen.—

[Aside.

Out on the goddess !   She has flown again
Before my darling, blinding her sweet eyes.

[Hurries past the loom, pulling off the curtain.]

What is it, little Queen ?

*Helen*.

I 'm over it, good Æthra ; you may go.

[She rouses, to find Paris gazing at the figures in the loom.]

As it has always been ! my will is naught.
My heart is out, dropt, naked, in your hand,
Where you may turn it, look it round and round.

*Paris*.

Through the long hours I pleasured with the king
My fancy, too, dwelt on the absent one,
To call her up.   Your task, to mine, was light ;
My fancy flagged, most miserably failed.

*Helen*.

If ever in my life I held resolve,
Clung to it long as I could hold it, I
Have done so now.   I vowed to live love down,

36

Or free it, as there, that it might fly away ;
I meant, believe me, none should ever know it.


### Paris.

Dear Queen ! my soldier's hand laid soft on this
White hand, love's lily, drooped in evening sleep,
I swear, as on the altar of the gods,
My will is weak as yours ; my will, ere this
Stubborn as the grim stone in Ilion's wall.
We are as children, you and I ; both helpless.


### Helen.

A child am I ; alas ! have ever been
A child, a cast leaf on the uncaring wind.
I pray you, woo me not, but teach me, Paris ;
Oh, tell me what I do, and why I do it !
Instruct me ; for you see I cannot hide
It longer.   My love is but too plain.   There is
No need of wooing ; teach me, Paris, teach me !


### Paris.

Know, then, I could not win you of myself ;
The man was never born, nor shall the man
Be born, that much a god.   The Queen of Love
Must win my queen.

### Helen.

        I knew it was no dream ;
She circled thrice your chariot as you came.
Her now I feel, her breath upon my face,
Her heart against my own.   I float between
A waking and a sleep; I swim in bliss.

### Paris.

My heart believes it, daughter of the gods.
This much I know for truth :
She promised me the fairest woman born,
She promised I should have whom now I have,
Of earth or Heaven the sweetest, sweetest Love.

### Helen.

Teach me it every hour, Love, while I live,
Too sweet a lesson to be sooner learned.

### Paris.

The tale I told you when we met, was but
Half told ; I 'll end it, now.  The Queen of Love—
A thing she needed not to do to make
Me more her slave, for I was prostrate fallen
Before her—she, I say, soft in my ear
Whispered these haunting words : '' For this fair
     gift
Will I bestow a fairer.  Love has bred

'Mong men the wonder of her kind, supreme
For beauty, first for all that flesh can wear
Of Heaven, peerless alike in seasons gone
And in the unnumbered summers yet to come.
She is my special charge, more dear to me
Than dearest daughter to a mortal mother.
Her will I lead you to ; her loveliness,
Yea, all her love, is yours.''

### Helen.

Goddess, forgive me, unworthy of your care,
My feeble blame !   You will forget it all ;
For you know all my past.   Now lift I praise
Of a full heart, which thankfully would stop
Were 't not to throb beyond this perfect hour.

### Paris.

Nay, nay, our cup is not yet filled ; the future
Shall pour it fuller yet.   Turn to the past,
My Love, my peerless Love,
And briefly tell me what it was, that I
May set against that night the day to be.

### Helen.

It seems so far away, now ; and so near
But yesterday !  I 'll tell it as best I may.
When I had years enough to know how dread

39

A thing is death, a plague fell on the land,
And we must make our costliest offering.
Thus early weighed on me the curse of beauty.
They seized me ; yea, my father dragged me forth,
The darling of his heart.　They braided up
My long, bright hair, the plaything of the winds
That loved to chase me on the sunny hills ;
They bound it up, and, there, among the flowers,
Among my own wild flowers, they bared the
　　knife
To spill my blood into their pitying faces.

*Paris.*

Horror unspeakable!　Say on, say on.

*Helen.*

I closed my eyes to the clear blue above,
And knew no more.　When I awoke, I was
At home again, and they were weeping round
　　me,—
Weeping for joy that I was spared.　It seems,
The wicked knife, raised, glittering in the sun,
Fierce swept an eagle down, and with her talons
Tore it from the bad hand, and sunk it in
A heifer's side.　The stricken creature bled,
The plague was stayed, and my poor life was saved.

40

### Paris.

O Aphrodite, if poor human might
The least can aid your sovereign will, henceforth
Take thou my all for this one precious deed !

### Helen.

It is so far away.   So close 't was, once,
So close and killing !  now almost forgot.

### Paris.

Feel me, my drowsy Love ;  I do not say
Awake.   Sleep on, and sweeter be the sleep ;
But know my arms are round you, and our bliss
Is not a dream.  This kiss, though you slept sound
As any sleep in graves, this must you feel,
And know it mine.   I will not interrupt
You save with kisses;  speak, say on, say on.

### Helen.

A child short-robed, and castanet in hand,
I danced among the dancers in the Temple —
To-morrow will I take you to the place —
When on us broke resistless Theseus, with him
His friend Pirithoüs ;  and I again
Was seized, and borne away to a stranger-land.
The gift most dangerous of the gifts of Heaven
Again had cursed me ;  and so young yet !  Oh,

Take back poor beauty's praise, and give it pity!
They hid me at Aphidnæ, in her care
Whose breast has been my pillow to this day,—
My faithful Æthra.

### Paris.

Æthra! I know her, now;
She is great Theseus' mother.   Next our goddess
And god-born Helen love I hoary Æthra.

### Helen.

Ay, she had screened me from Pirithoüs,
Had held me safe against her son himself.
As it befell, the test went not so far;
For, as the eagle swept to me, at home,
Came rushing down into the stranger-land
My noble brothers, they that sailed with Jason,
Immortal Polydeuces and Castor, sons
Of Zeus, on whose dear heads he set the stars,
And gave them fame white as the steeds they rode
To ravage Attica from end to end,
And bring me back to Sparta.   What has been
Since then — let it go by.   If I should speak
Of all, 't would be with blame for those of whom
I would speak well or nothing.   Here I am,
Despite the winds of fate;
Yes, Paris, I am here, the same cast leaf.

But something says 't will be a gentle gale
That takes me next; I pray for it, and think
'T will be.    I think, next time, my heart will float
With me, and we shall have a happy journey.
My loving brothers, every other day
Returning from the darkness into light,
Guardians of all that wander to and fro,
Will go with me; and you, my King, will go
With me, and I shall pass on ways of peace,
Ways all unknown thus far, but opened, now,
And smoothed for me, by her, the sovereign god-
          dess,
By her, dear Love, and you.


*Paris.*

You, Oreades, who glide through the wild trees,
And charm the warring mountains with your
          motion ;
You, Nereides, who gleam in the green sea,
Who toll the bell swung in the coral tower,
And trip the mossy round with Thetis ; you
Whose hands unlatch the skyey windows, and
          loose
The rain and sunshine ; ay, and you who wake
The world from her white slumber, and sow her
          couch

With blossoms, sweetest Hours and sweetest
    Airs ; —
Come, fairest, all, of earth and sea and sky,
And look upon yourselves, and see how small
A part you are of her, my Spartan Helen.


### Helen.

Say on, sweet Paris ; let me not awake.


### Paris.

If, swallows, you lead hither soft-eyed Spring,
Till Helen come comes never golden Summer ;
Her dwelling's here, here in this yellow hair.
Should Helen, in Tethys' place, receive the sun
When he would slumber, there 'd be no more
    day ;
Once on her breast, he would never rise again.
O golden Queen, forget the past ! look on
The present, which but ushers in the years
When men nor sowed nor reaped, yet all the
    world
Was as a garden ; when the brooks ran milk,
And up and down the air grew melody, —
The years men thought were gone, the golden
    years,
Led back, glad captives, in this golden hair.

## Helen.

Æthra! Paris! oh! oh! where have I been,
And am come back to this?

## Paris.

           Swift horror seams
Across your smooth girl-brow. Sweet Queen, we
    are
Beyond the reach of trouble, risen above it,
As birds from the earth, ay, as the clouds that mate
In the mid-azure. Ah, forgetful Helen!

## Helen.

A file of ghosts went past me, glided by,
Dim shapes of men yet dwelling in bright Hellas,
Great in the land, their wrathful helmets blazing,
Their corselets horrible with blood. I knew
The spectres; once before they came, no phantoms,
Resolved, each one, to take me home, his bride.
Far as Euripus' bank I followed them,
And saw them launch their slender, vengeful boats,
And speed along the Ægean northward. Fly,
O precious Paris! ere it be too late.

## Paris.

By all the might of mighty gods, if Paris
Set forth, to-night, Charon will be his oarsman.

There 's danger?    At a sign from me such men
Will quit their boats, and dash up from the strand,
As soon shall tame for us the haughty ghosts ;
When, from among their tumbled bodies, Helen
Will I lift up, and, with her in my arms,
Walk over them, and point ship-beaks for Ilion.

### Helen.

Dumb Menelaus, groping through the house
From room to room, holding in his great hands
The things I wore — I see him !   Now, he turns
From them to Agamemnon, whose huge breast
Is heaving horribly, broad as Poseidon's :
I cannot bear it longer.

#### Enter Æthra.

### Æthra.

Peace, silly children!   Let your elder speak,
Who, years ago, faced that same god Poseidon,
Nor feared him more than she fears now the ghosts
You talk of.   You have slept and waked.   It is
A way all children have, being but nature.
I am a mother, children, Theseus' mother ;
Two golden heads make not this old white head.
Peace, pretty babes, my hand will lead you home.
Paris, my son, 't is willed you should bear off

My daughter, Helen.   Whether alive or dead
Is not declared ; that lies, my son, with you.
Do you stir not, but wait to face the king,
You put that gentle head in peril worse
Than fate has woven for 't yet.   Take her, while now
You may, unharmed; house her in Ilion's hold,
Then, then return to tell what you have done.
The journey back, forsooth, will not be long ;
As you toward Greece, so Greece will move toward
      you.
Ay, she may meet you so far north that Helen
Can watch the brawl, safe in her Thracian tower.


*Paris.*

What say you? Take her so ! take Helen so !


*Helen.*

If I be not most honorably won,
Then love 's a liar, and there is no truth ;
But if true love speak truth, know I am won
Most fairly.   And if my wish have any weight,
And you would sometime take me, Paris, take
Me now.

*Paris.*

Hold that head up, a mark for scorn !

47

### Helen.

If scorn do point at me, 't will point because
Of what has been before this honest hour.
Go I or stay, I am not his, but yours ;
I never was the king's.
The shame is hers that falsely stays, not hers
That goes, bold only to be false no longer.
And yet so dread the shapes that vex my thought,
I pray you, go without me.   If alone
You go, or we set forth together, let
It be to-night.

### Æthra.

Stick to your loving, babes ;
There is no other logic straight as love's.
The creature does not breathe who would pronounce
Him wrong whose hand had snatched this miracle
From her own mother's arms ;
No wind shall ever bring the voice of blame
For Helen or the husband of her love.
My own boy Theseus, Prince, pounced on her once,
And haled her from the temple.   That was robbery ;
Yet all forgave it.   I myself forgave it.
But to forgive was not to make her his ;
The high gods bred and held her for another.
Love's day is come ;  and if you take her not
This night from damnéd Sparta, I say, now,

To your pale face, I will myself set out
With her, alone, and go and stand with her
Before old Priam ; nor tell him half the story
Ere he shall shake his years off, and, the might
Of youth once more upon him, brand his darling
The very basest 'mong his Thracian slaves.

Night. Paris and Helen are engaged in a finger-game, which
Helen invented to play with Paris. Æthra watches them,
herself unobserved.

*Æthra.* [Aside.
The storm is past, no cloud in all the sky ;
I cannot think that ever tempest was,
So fair the heaven of love, now. —Goddess, thine
Indeed is might, yea, sovereign might and grace !

*Helen.*

Could I but learn how dull you are at learning,
I should not try to teach you. You have lost
A twenty kisses in as many minutes.

*Paris.*

Is this the finger ?

6                    49

*Helen.*

That 's the very one

You lost on last.

*Paris.*

Then will I play it — so.

*Helen.*

You kissed before you played.

*Paris.*

Well, now I 've played.

*Helen.*

And kissed me out of turn.

*Paris.*

This takes it back.

*Helen.*

You cannot take it back.

*Paris.*

No? Then here 't is.

*Helen.*

I say again, it is a finger-game,
Not played with lips.—Was that the watcher's
signal?

#### *Paris.*

I 'll look, for one more kiss.

#### *Helen.*

I 'll look myself.

*Helen leaves the room, Paris following.*

#### *Paris.*

'T is a kind service. I will kiss you for 't.

#### *Æthra.*

Where now 's the king, and where is Salamis,
Where aught my pretty ones so hung on once?
All clean forgot: the goddess has her way.
So shone my girl's soft eyes when, back at Athens,
I used to tell her of Gorgo and Lamia.
Oh, it is worth my woes, worth all my bonds,
To look on this! Antic as nimblest fawns,
They frisk it to the chariot.— Dapple joys
Of Aphrodite, she will tend you well.
Soon as you mount, the waiting mist will fold,
And shut you safely from the peeping Spartans.
The very horses know their delicate errand;
The stallions, wont to neigh and prance as though
They rolled their wild eyes on Aurora's mares,
Now barely move their shiny sides for breath,
And every hoof is fixed as it were nailed

To the hard Spartan ground.  And I've helped, too,—
The king's fool-slaves have I drugged well with wine;
They will not wake till we be far at sea.
Boy Paris bade me go, and have my freedom ;
I will not take it till I see my bird
In her white cage, all safe in strong-walled Ilion.
Farewell to Lacedæmon !
When next a-hunting goes the hunter-king
'T will be a hunt with echoes will scud round
The circuit of the seas.  Farewell, once more,
Farewell to Lacedæmon !
Dark are the ways of men ; most brief are joys,
And of brief joys, is love, alas ! the briefest.
My dears, who dream so deep, must wake again ;
Tempest shall drive, and the wild shock of war
Shake down dream-builded bliss.  So let it be.
Love's hour is brief, but oh, that hour ! that hour !

# HOMERIC EXPERIMENTS

NOTE. These experiments are based on the English verse and prose of several translators; to whom, especially to Messrs. Lang, Leaf, and Myers, is here offered most humble apology.

# CHRYSES BEFORE AGAMEMNON

*(Opening of Book I )*

Sing, Goddess, crossed Achilles' brooding anger,
The wrath that worked the ruin of Achaia,
Brought on her all the many, many woes
Whereunder sank her noble souls to Hell,
Their bodies left upon the fateful field,
Carrion, to glut the vultures and the dogs ;
Sing the long-following horrors sent of Heaven,
Wroth for Atreides and Achilles' broil.
Which was it, 'mong the gods, that set them on?
The son that fair-haired Leto bore to Zeus,
He 't was, stirred up against the king, that smote
The host with a sore plague, and through the camp
Stalked awful death, for the dishonor done
His priest, white-haired old Chryses, whom he
 loved.

Now Chryses, both his old hands full of gifts,
Had wandered to the hollow ships to buy
His daughter back.   Upon his golden staff,

Wreathed with Apollo's chaplet, he leaned, and
    prayed
The Achaian people, crying on their chieftains:
" O kings, and ye well-greavéd warriors all,
Now, by the blesséd gods, may ye lay waste
The strong-walled town and get ye to your ships
And set off home in safety; only her
Take not.  Lo, costly gifts I bring; these take,
And leave my child to me.  So shall ye find
Sure favor in the eyes of him I serve,
Apollo, lovéd of the Lord of Heaven."
And all the people heard the old man gladly,
And they would take the ransom; only one
Stood out, the son of Atreus, Agamemnon.
Ruthless was he, and roughly made he answer:
" Stake not too much, old man, upon thy staff
And chaplet; get thee gone; let me not find thee
Among the hollow galleys any more.
For I 'll not free her; henceforth her home is Argos,
That far from kin and country; there, where wait
Her loom and her fair bed, her bed and mine.
Prate not, but go while yet 't is well with thee."

So spake he, and the good old man shrank back,
And crept away, and with bowed head passed on
Along the shore of the loud-sounding sea.

# HELEN ON THE TOWER

*(Book III)*

AND lovely, long-robed Helen answered him :
" I see the other Greeks with glancing eyes,
The great Achaians, I could name them all ;
But two I cannot find, two mighty ones
And valiant, Castor, conqueror of horses,
And Polydeuces, battler hand to hand,
My brothers, whom my own high mother bore.
They came not up from pleasant Lacedæmon,
Or else they sailed up in the hollow ships,
But stand, and watch the battle from afar,
Lest they should hear the evil things men say
Of me, given over to mockery and scorn." —
She said ; but both were fast asleep in death,
Back in their own dear land, fair Lacedæmon.

# MEETING OF THE DANAANS AND TROJANS

*(Book IV)*

As when, wild on the ever-roaring shore,
The wind out of the west rakes up a wave,
Draws, draws it up, and tumbles it, bellowing, on
The rock-butts, spuming to the precipice-top,
So rose and smote the Danaan battalions.
Only the captains spoke; the men rushed dumb,
As there were not a voice among them all;
Silent they came, and shining in their armor.
Not so the Trojans; they came on with clamor
Thick as the bleat of ewes, at milking-time,
Mewed in the rich man's pen, calling their lambs;
With all this noise came on the Trojan host.
For they had migrated from many lands,
And were of divers tongues.   Some Ares pricked
To war, and some gray-eyed Athene urged,
While others Terror goaded, Fright, and Strife,
Forever furious, sister and fit mate
Of murderer Ares, she that standeth squat
At first, and after stretches up her head

Heaven high, while yet her feet hold fast the ground.
She, ranging through the ranks, now hurried hot
The general rage, and set the battle on.

And it was battle.  Ox-hide shield on shield,
Targe griding targe, brass clanging brass, the dart,
Spike, spear fast clashing, might wild hurled on
     might—
The wide air rattled with it and the shouts
And death-groans, and the grasses swum in blood.

# HECTOR TO ANDROMACHE

*(Book VI)*

THEN answered her he of the glancing helm :
" All this, my wife, I think on, but bethink
Me, too, of all the scorn would cover me,
Shamed by famed Ilion's princes and the women
Of Ilion, raimented in trailing robes,
If so I skulk, and shun the front of war.
It must not be.   My very soul abhors it ;
For, from my youth up, it hath been my wont
To lead the fight, ay, in the van to strike
For hoary Priam's honor and mine own.
The future frights me not ; and this although
It shall not fail, but surely come to pass,
That goodly Ilion shall lie low, her head
Bowed in the dust, and Priam's old white head,
And all that lift for him the princely spear.
Yet not for this great woe my breast is torn
With anguish ; not for Hecabe, my mother,
Neither for Priam, my good father old,
Nor for my many brothers, all so brave,

And all foredoomed,—Oh, not for these my soul
Dies out within me, but for thee, the day
The brazen-mailed Achaian comes, and thou
Must rise and follow him.
Thereafter shalt thou bide with him at Argos,
And ply the alien loom, and bring for him
To drink, dipping the water wells, Messeïs
Or Hypereia, evilly entreated,
Doing his bidding and the will of fate.
And men shall look on thee, and see thy tears,
And say, " She once was Hector's, his that led
To fight the haughty conquerors of the horses
When wild the war was round the walls of Ilion."
So they will point thee out, in that dread day,
And fresh thy tears shall gush, for that thy bonds
Are grievous, and the man would rend them off,
Thy Hector, he, thy husband, is no more.

# ACHILLES TO ULYSSES

*(Book IX)*

AND shall I counsel with him? shall I give
Myself in any wise to him that could
Bespeak me fair and play me false?   No more;
Once is enough; now let him go his ways.
And he may go in peace; I take no man
To task whose head just Zeus hath touched and
    emptied.
Nor can I scorn him, fallen; hence on his gifts
Must heap my hate.   Ten times, ay, twenty times
What he has now or may hereafter have,
Though it should mount so high 't would pass in
    worth
Orchomenus and hundred-gated Thebes,
Each gate so broad, two hundred warriors, horse
And chariots, plunge in 't at once, nor choke it;
Yea, this, with gifts dealt out as the infinite sands,
I would not stoop to look on.   To right the past
Will cost yet dearer Atreus Agamemnon.
As for his daughter, did she shine before me,

Another Aphrodite, skilled withal
To tend the loom with her of the gray eyes,
She would not tempt me. Let him choose a man
More fit for her than I, more like a king.
When I would marry, I will look to Peleus ;
Do the gods but bring me home again, himself,
My father, will name the one his son shall wed.
In Hellas and in Phthia many a prince
Has fairest daughters—yes, and cities with them ;
And I may take my choice. In days bygone,
Full oft my heart was moved to take to me
A wife, and have my peace and joy at home,
Have all old Peleus hath, my honored father.
For happy life is all :
The treasure-store of broad-wayed Ilion ere
The sons of the Achaians came, her hoard
With that behind the Darter's marble door
Locked, there, in rocky Pythos,
Were nothing, weighed with life and peace and joy.
Tripods and cattle, horses auburn-maned,
Are his that wills to take them ; but when once
The life is out, the breath slipt through, well past
The teeth, what man of all shall bring it back ?
I know my fate, for she hath told it me,
My mother, silver-footed Thetis. Toward
My death there run two ways : if I wait on
To waste great Ilion, then my fame shall live,

But I myself am lost ;
Do I draw off, and fly this idle war,
Then shall my memory perish, but myself
Shall have enduring days, nor come to death
Till he shall meet me kindly in mine age.

And you, too, would I counsel to draw off,
And turn your prows toward home ; for Ilion's
    towers
Will not bow down to you, since Zeus doth hold
Them up against the world.— You have my answer,
Which, as befits your office, plain deliver,
And bid the Grecian leaders fix upon
A better way to save the hollow ships
And them that steered them hither.  On the way
Ye talked of think no longer ; it has failed.
But Phœnix, let him bide with me, to-night,
That on the morrow — should he will to go
With me, not otherwise — we may set out
For Phthia, Phthia our belovéd land.

# HERA IN HER CHAMBER

*(Book XIV)*

A<small>ND</small> straight she came up to her chamber, planned
And fashioned by her darling son Hephæstus,
Built with the massive doors, and secret bolt
No hand but hers could draw; hither she came,
And entered in, and closed the golden door.
And precious ointment she put on, and laved,
And made her lovely body without stain;
Nor stinted aught the smooth ambrosial oil
Of searching perfume, but one drop of which,
Spilled on the floor where the immortals walk,
Sets wandering sweetest odor up and down
The air throughout the earth and endless heaven.
So did the joy of Zeus exalt her beauty;
Then dressed with her white hands the blessèd
     hair
Forever flowing from her fragrant head.
And down she took the gown Athene made her,
The pleasant-smelling robe with delicate shapes
A-dancing out and in the shifting film,

And clad her in it, and looped it at the throat
With clasps of gold, and girt her girdle on,
Her belt with many tassels ; in her ears
She hung the swinging earrings, triple-gemmed,
Alive with fires that flickered every way ;
Then over her, down all the heavenly splendor,
She showered the veil, as of the morning sun-
    beams,
New-woven, unworn till now,
And tied the sandals on her shining feet.

# ACHILLES MOUNTS THE WAR CHARIOT

*(End of Book XIX)*

Aɴᴅ forth he drew his father's heavy spear,
Pond'rous and strong, no other hand could hold,
The spear that waited till he came to wield it,
Achilles ; Cheiron from a peak of Pelion
Brought it, and gave it to his honored father
For warrior's slaughterdom. And they, too, stirred,
The men Automedon and Alcimus,
Who put the shining harness on the horses —
The collars and the glossy straps, the bits
Which glittered in their jaws — and tossed the
    reins
Back to the solid chariot. In his hand
The lash, as 't were a meteor streaming, now
Automedon sprang up behind the team,
And after him Achilles, in his armor,
Peer of the Lord of Light, Hyperion,
And on his father's horses terribly
He called : '' Xanthus and Balius, you that boast
The blood of swift Podarge, see to it

You bring your master back, when he would
     breathe
From battle! fly not off, and leave him there,
As late you left Patroclus, lying dead!"
And Xanthus, whose slim hoofs are as the wind,
Bowed down his head and answered, and his mane,
And the glory of his mane, was on the ground;
Even so he bowed and answered, for sweet speech
He had of Hera, her of the white arms:
"Dread son of Peleus, verily once more
Will we two bring thee back, but know that death
Is nigh thee; not through us, but at the hands
Of them the during gods and ruthless Fate.
For not because we two were loth, or slack
In anywise, did Ilion strip away
Patroclus' arms, and rob his noble body;
It was that other, great among the gods,
The son of Leto of the lovely hair,
He felled him in the forefront of the fight,
And gave to Hector glory.   Not the wind
Out of the west hath nimbler feet than ours,
But thou art doomed, given over to be slain;
A god shall do it and a mortal man."
And here the Furies took away his speech,
And straight fleet-foot Achilles, filled with pain,
Lifted his voice: "Xanthus,
Must thou, too, stab at me?   It needeth not.

Too well I know that here shall be the end ;
Here shall I fall, far from my father dear
And my dear mother.   Nathless, ere I go
Shall many a Trojan throat be choked with war."
He said, and lashed the steeds ;
He cried, and to the front the chariot thundered.

www.ingramcontent.com/pod-product-compliance
Lightning Source LLC
Chambersburg PA
CBHW021524270326
41930CB00008B/1072